ON UNIVERSITY FREEDOM

in the Canadian context

KENNETH HARE

Published in association with
Carleton University
by University of Toronto Press

© University of Toronto Press 1968

Reprinted 2017

ISBN 978-1-4875-9135-9 (paper)

੧੨੧੨੧੨੧੨੧੨੧੨੧੨੧੨੧੨੧੨੧੨੧੨

ON UNIVERSITY FREEDOM
in the Canadian context

As Canadian universities grow increasingly expensive to
run and equip, and larger demands are made on federal and
provincial funds to meet these costs, the problem of the proper
relationship between government and universities becomes
immediate and pressing. This book, based on the Plaunt
Lectures given at Carleton University in 1967, discusses
the question at length. After comparing the American and
British systems, Dr. Hare suggests that the best solution in
Canada is for the universities themselves to form a strong
cooperative body and for the state to arm this body with
statutory instruments. Dr. Hare also considers the question
of the student unrest on campuses today and supports the
trend toward more student participation in university
administration. At a time when the problem of freedom
and control is one of the most controversial problems in the
academic world, this study will be of interest to all members
of that community, and to anyone in federal and provincial
politics.

KENNETH HARE received his B.Sc., Geography, from the
University of London and his Ph.D. from the University
of Montreal. He has taught at Manchester University and
at McGill where he was Professor and Chairman of the
Department of Geography from 1952 to 1962. From 1962
to 1964 he was Dean of Arts and Sciences at McGill after
which he was appointed Professor of Geography at King's
College, London. In 1966 he was appointed Master of
Birkbeck College in the University of London and in 1967
he was elected Fellow of King's College. He served as a
member of the Spinks Commission on the Development of
Graduate Programmes in Ontario Universities, 1966. He is
now President of the University of British Columbia.

੧੨੧੨੧੨੧੨੧੨੧੨੧੨੧੨੧੨੧੨੧੨੧੨

Those who expect to reap the blessings of freedom must, like men, undergo the fatigue of supporting it.

Tom Paine, *The American Crisis*, no. IV
Sept. 12, 1777

❀❀❀❀❀❀❀❀❀❀❀❀❀❀❀❀❀❀❀❀❀❀❀

PREFACE

This little book is based on the Allan B. Plaunt
Lectures that I gave at Carleton University, Ottawa,
on February 23 and 25, 1967, enlarged to take in
ideas raised in the discussions that followed.

I have tried to write as a Canadian, and for
Canadians. But I work for a British university, and
the whole tenor of my text is comparative. I am
exploring ideas that have had a longer history outside than inside Canada. With any luck Canadians
will now be able to take them further than any other
English-speaking society, because Canada is, thank
God, the land of open questions. Long may it remain
so. Anyone who tries to live in two countries, as I
do, runs the risk of sounding bad-mannered in both.
I apologize if this has happened in the following
pages.

I must thank many friends for helping me. In
Britain I owe much to Sir Eric Ashby, from whom
I learned most of the underlying ideas. Sir Douglas
Logan and Sir John Wolfenden also commented
helpfully on the text. To Sir John, who bears a torch

for all academics as chairman of the University Grants Committee, I owe a special debt for the quizzical good humour with which he regarded my often critical remarks. In Canada Dr. J. W. T. Spinks read the text and made helpful suggestions, and in the United States I owe a similar debt to the Honorable Gustave O. Arlt. Madame M. M. Mount, who typed the spoken draft, commented pungently from a Québec standpoint. The final text was typed in London by Miss Joanna McKie.

Finally my very warm thanks to Carleton University, and especially to its President, for the invitation. Dr. Dunton read the text, but declined to censor it. I hope he may be forgiven for what I said.

F.K.H.

Birkbeck College
University of London
April 12, 1967

vi

꒜꒜꒜꒜꒜꒜꒜꒜꒜꒜꒜꒜꒜꒜꒜꒜꒜꒜꒜꒜꒜꒜꒜

CONTENTS

꒜꒜꒜꒜꒜꒜꒜꒜꒜꒜꒜꒜꒜꒜꒜꒜꒜꒜꒜꒜꒜꒜

1

THE THREAT

Being neither prophet nor pundit I am embarrassed to address an audience under such a high-sounding title as "On University Freedom." I would have chosen something humbler if events hadn't forced my hand. The first was the timing of President Dunton's invitation to give the Plaunt Lectures. He took me aside at a meeting in June 1966 of the Ontario university presidents with the Spinks Commission on the Development of Graduate Programmes in Ontario Universities of which I had the honour to be a member. He guessed, and the Commissioners strongly suspected, that the province would find some of our ideas hard to swallow, at least in so far as they dealt with government. So the question of university freedom was in both our minds. I jumped at the chance of arguing these questions in public, and at Carleton University of all places, under the noses of those Canadians who should bother most about the public freedoms. Let me start, then, by thanking the President for his invitation.

There was another compelling reason why I liked the idea of exploring these ideas in public. On February 1, 1966, the Honourable William Davis, Minister of University Affairs in the Ontario Government, delivered the Gerstein lecture at York University, Toronto. This was a remarkable address. The Minister knew just where the academic solar plexus lay and he punched it hard. He deserves a reply from someone outside the Ontario university

3

system, and I am going to presume to be that someone. I don't belong in this province, and cannot tell either the Minister or the universities what to do. But as a Spinks Commissioner I have seen all the Ontario universities, and have spent a year considering the problems raised by their expansion. I and my colleagues saw much to admire and to astonish, and some things that were magnificent. It was a tonic year for us all. But expansion cannot take place on this scale without bringing to a head the vital question: what should be the relation between the universities and the provincial government?

Of course this isn't just an Ontario problem: it has cropped up throughout the Western world as the universities have expanded. In Ontario the provincial exchequer now meets over half the operating costs of the universities, and a higher proportion of the capital costs. Clearly this is enough to set any government's pulse racing. Moreover the proportion is sure to rise. In Britain, for example, where public financing of nominally autonomous universities is also a major issue, the public share of total costs is even higher. In 1964–65 the British universities received in all $372 million in revenues, equal to about $2,400 per head of their 154,434 full-time students. No less than 72 per cent came as direct exchequer grants. Research grants and tuition fees, also primarily from public sources, contributed a further 11 and 8 per cent respectively. Endowment income accounted for less than 2 per cent.[1] The

1. UNIVERSITY GRANTS COMMITTEE, *Returns from Universities and University Colleges in Receipt of Exchequer*

4

British university system is thus almost entirely dependent on public moneys, and I see little likelihood that Canada will escape a similar fate. We are witnessing the transformation of university systems into services akin to the schools and hospitals —demanded by the voter as a public necessity.

It does not follow that he who pays the piper calls the tune, at least in civilized nations. But it is still usually the case, even in the highest-minded countries. In Ontario one can hardly blame Mr. Davis for hinting that he has some claim to call a few of the changes: the creation of eight new chartered universities since 1959 is a guarantee that a new relation with the provincial government will have to be worked out. This expansion is an extraordinary leap forward, an act of faith in the university world by the public at large; but it is also a dive into deep financial waters for the provincial treasurer. University education is getting more expensive as it gets more widespread. This is particularly true of research and graduate studies, without which a university cannot now exist. By 1975–76, the Spinks Commission reckoned, there would be 23,000 graduate students in the Ontario universities.[2] This enrolment alone guarantees an extraordinary rise in costs.

What marked Mr. Davis's address as of special

Grant, *Academic Year 1964–65* (London: H.M.S.O., Cmnd. 3106, 1966), Table 11.

2. J. W. T. SPINKS (Chairman), Commission to Study the Development of Graduate Programmes in Ontario Universities, *Final Report* (Toronto: Government of Ontario,

importance was that he got down to details, and asked specific questions. Since these are all relevant to my purpose, I shall briefly paraphrase them. He first asked whether the universities had really recognized the need for economy. Many people, he said, had suggested to him that this was not so. Among other things he instanced the favourable staff-student ratio in Ontario (1:14), and asked why California and Michigan could cope with ratios like 1:16 or 1:17 without apparent loss of standards. Coming from recent experience in Britain I find all these ratios unfavourable, but that is not the point here. What matters is that half the cost of running universities is in paying salaries, so that the Minister can fairly ask the question, even though he may find the answer unwelcome (as I am sure he will). This question reflects a growing unease in the minds of the well-informed in many countries. Can universities, which shun business methods, and resist public accountability, really be efficient? And is efficiency the same thing as economy of operation? How do you define it, when you are dealing with such intangibles as the sharpening of intelligence and the discovery of new knowledge?

Mr. Davis then turned his attention to the launching of new programmes and projects. Boards of Governors, he asserted, were apt (in some cases) to announce new medical centres, new faculties and new departments without prior discussion with the Government to see whether funds might be avail-

Dept. of University Affairs, 1966), Table IV. (Cited as *Spinks Report.*)

6

able. No university, he roundly declared, "by making prior announcements about its plans should believe that the Government is in any way committed to supporting those plans." The Government would retain the right to make such decisions in the light of the over-all needs of the Province. He also asked whether autonomous universities could curtail "the non-constructive aspects of competitiveness that now prevail among them." Competition was excellent, he contended, if it took the form of bold and really new ventures, of exciting new approaches to higher education. It was undesirable if it led to wasteful duplication of expensive facilities, or to competition between universities for publicly supported students.

The Minister also asked whether universities, with their tradition of autonomy, could "subordinate their individual ambitions if society, as a whole, would be better served by such action"? He chose as an example the questions of graduate work and library resources. He had heard constant and conflicting pleas on these subjects, and he was sure that the solution must lie "in co-operation and co-ordination; a willingness on the part of one university to share its facilities (libraries included) and, indeed, its staff with students of another. . . ." Equally he asked whether universities, supposing that they learned thus to co-operate with one another, could learn to co-operate with non-university institutions like technical and teachers' colleges. Without such co-operation he plainly feared for the future of post-secondary education in the Province.

These questions, publicly presented by one of

Canada's most effective politicians, are all very much to the point. They are vivid and fresh in Ontario, where university expansion is so recent and so remarkable. They are a little more familiar in some older jurisdictions. But they are real enough and relevant enough in any part of the free world to justify urgent discussion. And of course they are in fact being discussed, most of all by university men and women themselves. It is true that institutions sometimes seem to drag their feet, but their individual members are certainly concerned. No responsible academic can deny that Mr. Davis's questions deserve not merely answers but action on our part. And at once we are brought up against the question of freedom—the academic freedom that is one of the western world's remarkable achievements.

These are shark-infested waters, and if I swim in them I expect to feel a nip or two. Nevertheless I shall dive in, because my recent life has convinced me that the proper relation between universities and government is one of the really important political questions of the day. I have had to cross the Atlantic about once every six weeks during the past two years; I have worked as teacher, scientist, and administrator on both sides, and have served on the research councils of both Britain and Canada. In addition I am a graduate (*diplomé*) of the Université de Montréal, with its French roots, and am sympathetic to many of the ideals and methods of the United States universities. So I see, if I see at all, through comparative spectacles. Both sides of the Atlantic have something sensible to teach us—

and each other. I wish I could take back to Britain something of the capacity of Ontario, indeed of Canada generally, for getting new buildings up and new programmes launched; and I'd be popular in my university if I could teach the British the American art of generous giving. In the reverse direction, the British have hitherto been able to rely on much more respectful treatment by the state than have Canadian and American universities. The British universities have been protected, not because state interference is illegal, but because it has been thought unthinkable. These conventions, these largely unwritten guarantees, will no doubt grow here, too; in Britain they show signs of being no longer binding. The point is that I have lived in both climates, and try to see their relative merits. That is what I mean, in the context of these lectures, by seeing through comparative spectacles.

Academic freedom is part of the general freedom of liberal democratic societies; but it is also something special. A case has to be made for it even in the most enlightened countries. There is nothing self-evident about the right to teach whom, what, when and how one wants. The proof that academic freedom is a desirable end is empirical. The best universities—those that pursue and spread their learning most effectively—seem to be those that govern themselves. It is true that we can justify such freedom on other grounds. A democratic society must try to limit governmental regulation and control; the more its institutions are free and independent, the more effective is democracy itself, and the more true freedom remains to its citizens. A state that tries to cherish such free institutions will usually put the universities high on the list: for universities are, or ought to be, not only a main home of knowledge and wisdom, but also the intellectual conscience of the nation. Nevertheless the practical case for freedom is that free universities are better than servile universities, and hence they serve the public interest.

Those who make this claim point to the unfree for their evidence; for we know what unfreedom is. Robbins puts it like this: "an academic institution is unfree if its members are forced to confine their teaching to modes and creeds in which they do not believe, if appointment depends, not on excellence of qualification and performance but on membership of a political party or of a church, and if the search for truth and values is subordinated to the exigencies of particular ideologies."[3] And of course we can see that unfreedom about us in many places: in Nazi Germany yesterday, in the Soviet Union, Spain and South Africa today. We recognize it closer to home in those few institutions which still apply a religious test at their gates. It has had its victims in Ontario, though miraculously the clouds have rolled away in the last few years. In such unfree environments distinction may still be achieved, but in a narrow intellectual frame dictated by the state

3. LORD ROBBINS, *Of Academic Freedom* (London: Oxford University Press, for the British Academy, 1966), p. 11.

or church. Technical competence may be achieved, too, as in the Marxian universities. But I don't doubt that the free universities of the West, and especially of the English-speaking countries, are immensely stronger. Let me quote, not for the last time, some words of Eric Ashby delivered before an audience in the splendid but beleaguered University of the Witwatersrand: "To forbid the student to learn where and what he will, or the teacher to teach whom and how he will, is to put a curb on the hazardous adventure of thinking, and a nation where thinking is rationed simply cannot survive in today's world."[4] I'm forced to ask: is this really true? The Soviet Union and South Africa have had a good run for their money while denying this sort of conclusion; and General Franco has remained quite unimpressed. But, true or false, this claim about freedom remains our liberal creed. We assume it here, and await the further proofs that we hope will appear.

Academic freedom has two aspects, related but distinct. There is the freedom claimed by the individual scholar. And there is the autonomy of the university to which he belongs. I am tempted to say that the fight for individual freedom is almost won in Canada, as it has long been in Britain. In the Ashby dictum I have just repeated you may have recognized the Germanic twins of *Lehrfreiheit* and *Lernfreiheit*. We have been zealous in defending the

---

4. SIR ERIC ASHBY, *Universities under Siege* (Johannesburg: University of the Witwatersrand, 1962), p. 8.

11

teacher's *Lehrfreiheit*—his right to teach as he wants—and have almost achieved it in the English-speaking world. The *Lernfreiheit* of the student is not as healthy: we dragoon our young in middle-aged confidence that we know what is good for them. But at least we let them pick their own universities and main subjects; and there is far more *Lernfreiheit* about Canadian degrees, with their high elective content, than there is about the martial discipline of a British honours school. Leaving aside this question of the student's rights, then—though I shall come back to it—I think we can say that in most places the freedom of the scholar from his university "administration," from pressure groups beyond the gates, and from the interference of the state, has been largely won.[5]

But I am not so sure about the second aspect, the freedom of universities as institutions—their so-called autonomy. And herein lies the reason for these lectures. If autonomy is a good thing, we must try to preserve it. Doing so will depend on waking up to the dangers that face us—that face us not only in Ontario, but everywhere in the English-speaking world, not least in Britain. I shall argue later that these dangers—let us call them threats—are as much internal as external, as much due to our own unpreparedness as to any dragons in Queen's Park, Whitehall or on Capitol Hill. In

---

5. I was sorry that Dr. Frank Underhill, now of Carleton University, was not present when I said these words, because of ill health. Few men have done more to win this fight than he has.

spite of incessant warnings, I believe that the university community, here and overseas, does not yet see this threat clearly. In Canada the professor's main concern has been with his own freedom and with his rights inside his institution: the enemy has been the governor or trustee, not the state. When I was the president of a branch of the Canadian Association of University Teachers, eleven years ago, the internal government of universities was our main worry, together with our anxiety to increase financial support from the federal government. And I'm sure that the average governor, nettled by this attitude, and habituated to the authoritarian atmosphere of upper management in Canadian industry, would probably have called the professor the university's chief liability. The representative document of this period was Willson Woodside's book *The University Question*, significantly sub-titled *Who Should Go? Who Should Pay?*[6] It dealt with money, with what the universities ought to teach, with the level of student intake, with where to get professors, with relations with industry. The decision-makers, in Woodside's eyes, were the governors and presidents: the professors still emerged as employees. And he was right, as a good journalist usually is. In his book he did not suggest that university freedom was anything to lose any sleep over.

These attitudes have coloured Canadian thinking

---

6. WILLSON WOODSIDE, *The University Question* (Toronto: Ryerson Press, 1958), 199 pp.; foreword by F. Cyril James, pp. vii–viii.

to the present time, and the issues are not yet dead. The great documents of the past two years have been the Duff-Berdahl report on internal university government[7] and the Bladen commission report on university finance.[8] The Duff-Berdahl report is a statement of the liberal position on internal government and of the extent to which Canadian practice falls short of it. The tenth chapter deals with the relations between universities and provincial governments, but this discussion is secondary to the authors' real purpose, which is to accelerate the reform of internal government. Considering its joint sponsorship, we can think of the report as the culmination of the long struggle of the academic community to run its own internal affairs: to ensure that academic policy flows upwards from the faculty meeting, and not downwards from the board room. Reforms along Duff-Berdahl lines have already penetrated the better Canadian universities, and the change has produced much goodwill: the president tends to be as much the faculty's man as the governors' and the suspicion between professor and

---

7. SIR JAMES DUFF and R. O. BERDAHL, *University Government in Canada*, report of a commission sponsored by the Canadian Association of University Teachers and the Association of Universities and Colleges of Canada, (University of Toronto Press, 1966), 97 pp. (Cited as *Duff-Berdahl Report.*)

8. VINCENT W. BLADEN (chairman), *Financing Higher Education in Canada*, report of a commission established by the Association of Universities and Colleges of Canada, (University of Toronto Press, 1965), 104 pp.

governor is dwindling. But let me repeat—this issue is not dead. There are Canadian universities that will have to be dragged, kicking and screaming, into Confederation's second century. Nevertheless I am sure that the battle is nearly won, and that the dinosaurs will soon be seeking their last bed of pitch.

The Bladen report, another crucial document, is the culmination of the other main issue of the decade: enough money. To quote Cyril James in the foreword to Woodside's book: "But if the people of Canada fail to provide *at once* [James was writing in 1957] the additional financial resources that are needed to enlarge teaching staffs and to construct additional buildings, the price of this expansion in student enrolment will be the standardization of university education in this country at a more mediocre level."[9] Carleton's splendid new buildings, and the other spanking new campuses elsewhere in Ontario, are evidence that the people of Canada seem to have risen to James's challenge. When I revisit McGill these days I reflect that the mainly French Canadian provincial government seems to have treated my old academic home more generously than the British state does the University of London. Looking in from outside, I find the changed situation in Canada remarkable, and can only praise the response to the need. Bladen's commission made it clear that great efforts will still be needed to maintain progress, and I have heard

---

9. WOODSIDE, *The University Question*, p. vii. The bracketed phrase is mine.

15

President Dunton say that the next decade will be very difficult. But here again I feel the main battle has been won: the public admits that it has really got to pay for higher education. The argument is about how much, and by what means.

I come now to my central point. "How much" is a figure so large that university expenditures are becoming one of the biggest items in the country's provincial budgets. In Saskatchewan (whose 1966–67 provincial budget for all purposes is smaller than that of the University of California) the university system gets nearly 10 per cent of the public purse. The ratio is lower in the large provinces, but it is still high. Bladen's estimates for the next decade[10] make stark reading:

ESTIMATED AND PROJECTED TOTAL PUBLIC EXPENDITURE ON UNIVERSITIES AND STUDENT AID			
	1964–65 (*estimate*)	1970–71 (*projected*)	1975–76 (*projected*)
Millions of 1965 dollars	355	1,112	1,704

Thus in eleven years the cost to the federal and provincial governments of the national university system is expected to rise fivefold. How in the face of this can we hope to ensure that the academic

---

10. BLADEN, *Financing Higher Education in Canada*, Table XI, p. 36.

16

community retains its institutional autonomy? Can Canadian politicians, or indeed politicians anywhere, face expenditure on this scale without claiming detailed control over its use?

Obviously this is not simply an Ontario problem. In Canada it is nationwide; every province is seeking, ought to seek, or has sought, a proper solution for it. Outside Canada it is literally Western worldwide, and it must exist even in the Communist block in altered form. But in few places does the problem present itself as acutely as in Ontario, for in few places has anyone had the will and the resources to expand universities so rapidly and on so large a scale. Mr. Davis stressed this point in presenting the 1966–67 estimates of his Department of University Affairs to the Ontario legislature.[11] He compared the Province's record in capital projects with the much smaller current capital efforts in Michigan and Ohio. He might well have included the United Kingdom, no laggard when it comes to university affairs. He added that the contribution to total operating revenues coming from Queen's Park has risen from $23.3 million in 1961–62 to $81.2 million in 1966–67—corresponding to 35 per cent and 54 per cent of total revenues. With federal aid added in, the total public contribution to the operating revenues of Ontario universities becomes $121

---

11. WILLIAM G. DAVIS, Minister of University Affairs, Statement before the Fourth Session of the Twenty-Seventh Ontario Legislature, Toronto, June 16, 1966 (Toronto: Queen's Printer).

million—which, however, is no more than Harvard's annual budget.

There is, of course, one very simple and quite wrong solution. Universities can be absorbed by the state, and run as part of the national bureaucracy. One can even develop healthy *Lehrfreiheit* within such a non-autonomous or servile system. This is true of France, where the old independent universities vanished with the *ancien régime*, to be replaced by a Napoleonic structure completely centralized in administrative matters. Frenchmen are not easily intimidated, and in few places will one hear more pungent criticism of a centralized system. But the criticism goes unheeded, as it washes over the monumentally thick skins of the Parisian bureaucrats. Let me quote the caustic Rector of the Université de Dijon, Dr. M. Bouchard:

Even if the Director-General [of higher education] is a Rector, a Dean or a University Professor, the departmental heads and officials at all levels who prepare decisions and transmit instructions are administrators—each dealing only with those questions for which he is particularly responsible. Between them they play the part of a Providence which examines everything, knows everything, prepares everything, arranges everything, whose intervention is as necessary for fixing a lecture hour or a new discipline as it is for equipping a laboratory, and which decides when the golden rain of subventions shall fall. In the corridors of the Ministry, one can watch the mendicant Rectors, Deans and Professors journeying from office to office much as in

Rome one sees the pilgrims moving from church to church in search of indulgences.[12]

If, as I hear rumoured, there are Québec intellectuals who wish to see the Napoleonic writ run in their universities, I hope they will ponder this *cri du cœur*. Nor do the German universities enjoy their similar bondage. Lord Robbins tells the story of the director of education in one of the West German *Länder*, who boasted that a rector couldn't switch the tiniest item of expenditure from one budgetary line to another without his office's permission. Robbins asked him if this ever caused resentment, whereupon he replied "Never!" But Robbins heard a muttered comment from behind the hand of a nearby young academic: "Because we are a set of sheep."[13]

The English-speaking countries have for the most part tried out a quite different device: the buffer committee. This is a respected body of intermediaries, trusted (in principle) by both academics and politicians. They have the job of assessing need, persuading the politicians to part with the money, and then distributing that money to the universities. There are two main species of this genus, both long-established. The British favour committees, which they name and discuss in a subfusc sort of way, and characteristically they depend on convention rather

---

12. M. BOUCHARD, "France," in *University Autonomy, Its Meaning Today* (Paper 7; Paris: International Association of Universities, 1965), pp. 59–60.

13. LORD ROBBINS, *Of Academic Freedom*, p. 11.

19

than on carefully formulated law. Many Americans prefer the concept of a Board of Regents, made up of distinguished citizens, carrying great public prestige, and supported by legislation. But the ideas, though different on the surface, are similar in principle, and often in execution. Not all jurisdictions employ the device of the buffer committee, but the idea is spreading as its merits become apparent. Ontario has such a committee, though it lacks a properly defined rôle. Québec may soon have one, but I confess I can no longer even guess what the Province intends as a lasting solution.

To make the buffer committee system work you have to pick the right committee, and you have to persuade universities and politicians alike to let it do the job. Exactly how you do this will depend on the jurisdiction you are in: there are no eternal verities in this down-to-earth business. You have to pick a formula that fits the local power-structure, and this varies surprisingly from country to country. Later in these lectures I shall look at one or two successful patterns. But before I do so I must look at the consequences to the university community of any system of massive public subsidy. Most of these consequences follow in any type of arrangement short of the fully state-centralized plan of Napoleon. To make the buffer system work we in the universities have to accept certain restrictions on our freedom—*and to impose these upon ourselves.*

The first is that we have got to admit, grudgingly or not, that the universities in a modern country form a system. They are not isolated individuals, able to go their own way without bothering about what their neighbours are doing. They together constitute a single system meeting a single public need. In Britain the universities are very much accustomed to this idea. Their system—the word recurs—of centralized admissions, for example, now universal for full-time undergraduates in England and Wales, enables a student to pick his university anywhere in the two countries and his local authority grant allows him to do so. He is under no obligation to go to his local campus, and in general he tries to avoid doing so. Hence all the universities are fully national in constituency. From this admission policy follow certain consequences. The universities have to spend much money on providing residences, and on organizing lodgings bureaux. The policy has raised the proportion of students in university residences from 28 to 32 per cent between 1953–54 and 1964–65, and in lodgings from 41 to 50 per cent. Students living in their own homes have fallen from 31 to 18 per cent in the same period.[14] The British have thus followed nationally a most expensive policy, based on the assumption that it is better for the students to go away from home than to commute from that home to a local university. It may be that this policy was wrong, and that the huge capital and operating sums necessary to implement it would have been better spent on laboratories, offices or classrooms. The point is, however, that it is a policy, executed with the aid of the University

14. University Grants Committee, *Returns* . . ., p. 1.

21

Grants Committee, bearing on all universities alike, and arising from concerted action by those universities acting as a system.

We all know that the academic tradition is highly individualistic. I remember a picture, I think in the *New Yorker*, of the UN headquarters in New York with all the flags of the nations flying one way, except for one lonely flag pointing the other way. It was the flag of the Soviet Union, but it might well have been that of Academe. We resist uniformity, change, external control, organization. We are not organization men, but cave-dwellers. And we are by nature competitive as societies, even tribal in characteristics. The mere thought that common action by our tribes in confederacy, like that of the Iroquois, might strengthen our hand, leaves us disdainful. Many of us will publicly deny this, but mentally admit it. Those who work at Carleton University do not, I suspect, cheer when another university gets money from some donor. In London as head of one college I keep a friendly but watchful eye on my colleagues in the other colleges. This is the natural atmosphere of the profession, student and teacher alike. To remember that we are colleagues in the same system with our competitors is not easy. The threat from within is in fact this individualism, this unwillingness to organize.

But to organize is now necessary, at least under conditions of central financing. If one spends public money one must spend it responsibly. And that means eliminating wasteful competition or duplication of facilities, judging demand, assessing social needs and seeing well into the future. All these require system-wide consideration and action. Taking the bulk of our income from a single public purse gives us no choice.

Of course this restriction on liberty of local decision, this need to co-ordinate, does not arise so forcefully if public money is not involved. Waterloo Lutheran breathes a fresher air than Carleton because it gets along without any help. The rich private universities can afford to be individualists. Harvard, Yale and Princeton can; so can a few others. Significantly, however, their actions show many signs of wishing to complement, and not to duplicate, the state university programmes. The reason is partly distaste for state university methods, but largely the trustees' convictions, reinforced by those of the professoriate, that wealth does not exempt one from public discipline and responsibility. In Britain, Oxford and Cambridge long ago became part of the national system. They have retained, because others have been willing to concede, much of their uniqueness, and they remain to some extent places apart. But they are national universities, dependent like the rest on public moneys, and responding like the rest as best they can to common public purposes.

Here in Canada the universities are only part way towards thinking of themselves as a system, or systems (if someone asserts that the francophone universities are separate). They were for long members or associates of the National Conference of Canadian Universities and Colleges, and, since federal aid became a reality, of its executive arm, the Canadian Universities Foundation—both succeeded since August 1, 1965, by the Association of Universities and Colleges of Canada. Meeting together nationally like the learned societies, the senior members of the Canadian universities have long mastered the art of joint consultation, and, let me add, of joint dissipation. Out of this habit has come a well-organized federal lobby—amazingly successful by non-Canadian standards—and a mechanism for distributing federal aid. But these bodies, valuable and praiseworthy though they have been, did not and cannot co-ordinate the Canadian university systems, because the universities must constitutionally deal with the provinces in which they find themselves.

Hence, under the pressure of financial need, the out-stretched palms of most presidents have had to turn towards their provincial capitals, and a new problem—new in some of the provinces, at any rate—arises: how to cope with the provincial government when it begins to dominate sources of academic revenue. For the Prairie Provinces this is *vieux jeu*, because they have always had provincial systems: and so it was in British Columbia until recently, when the complications of growth set in. In Ontario and Québec, however, where there are many universities, and where the provincial governments are deeply involved with private institutions, the problem is real and urgent. In the Maritimes the story is also complex, though not different in principle. But it is in Ontario, with fourteen provincially assisted yet autonomous universities, that the problem is classically posed—and it is here that academic history has got to be written in the next few years.

In talking of systems of universities, then, we inevitably mean provincial systems. The need to co-ordinate, to complement, not to duplicate, is most effective *within* a province, not across the nation, however regrettable this may be—and I do regret it. Our buffer committees will thus be provincial—I hope only in a constitutional sense. Clearly an Ontario system of universities is in being; there is a bureaucracy on University Avenue, a buffer committee, a vigorous minister and a massive commitment of funds—$803 million for capital alone in the period 1966–71, or an average of about $160 million per annum, three-quarters from the public purse. If you compare this, from a population of about 6 million, with the corresponding figure for Britain of about $180 million per annum from a population of 50 million, you realize the scale of that commitment. The British see themselves as a modest people, and one cannot deny that they have plenty to be modest about.

Now the decision-making process in the world of the Canadian universities is anything but systematic. It is individualistic at all levels: strong and opinionated presidents, aggressive boards, newly invigorated senates and faculty boards, locals of the C.A.U.T. All are habituated to the idea that initiative is local. In the ideal world of local autonomy the University —shall we say of Plantagenet or Alfred, because their names, so familiar to Ottawans, have a nice medieval flavour—decides to start up a programme of psephology. It does this, either because it has anxious politicians on its Board, or because some expert professor of psephology convinces the Senate that Platagenet or Alfred is the right place to teach it. The Board then raises the capital needed from local industry or other rich donors, and builds the new Institute: and funds are committed from general revenues to employ staff and run the building. So Plantagenet-Alfred is launched on a new academic venture. It is quite likely that the Senate and Board *will* have asked the questions: Does this institute meet a clear public demand? Is there a university down the road doing the same thing? If so, are we justified in competing? But I can only say that in my experience such conscience-trawling is not very effective. To quote Robbins again, this time his committee's report: "But it is unlikely that separate consideration by independent institutions of their own affairs in their own circumstances will always result in a pattern that is comprehensive and appropriate in relation to the needs of society. . . . There is no guarantee of the emergence of any coherent policy."[15] I agree, though I would have been blunter. Local initiatives will produce a coherent policy only if they are taken in the light of stated social needs. No forum exists in Canada whereby these needs can be formulated, and whereby the universities can judge these matters. And certainly there is no pro-

---

15. Committee on Higher Education (Lord Robbins, chairman), *Higher Education* (London: H.M.S.O., Cmnd. 2154, 1963), para. 719, p. 233.

vincial forum, unless, perish the thought, it is the Legislature.

This matter of co-ordination between universities has been a real issue in compact and much-evolved Britain, and I shall later say how the University Grants Committee tries to solve it. It is a major issue in Québec. I was a member of the McGill Senate for many years. It is a very good body, and during those years it set up many new programmes —for example, the Marine Sciences Centre, the Centre for Developing Areas and the Islamic Institute. In all cases we debated the merits of these proposals in a quite enlightened and public-spirited way, because we were pretty sure—and events proved us right—that we could get the money from special, non-governmental sources. But when it came to deciding admissions policies, and such matters as staff-student ratios, then we worked in a vacuum. And I may say with shame that as Dean of Arts and Science at McGill I never once had occasion to consult or to co-ordinate my Faculty's work with my opposite numbers at Sir George Williams or the Université de Montréal. In Québec it took a Royal Commission—the Parent Commission—to undertake fundamental thinking about educational policy. Such commissions pass into history. What is needed is a continuous forum that never stops debating the public stake in the universities. And in my view that forum should itself be an academic body.

What, in outline, do we need to plan in a university system? Obviously the least number of things possible. But even the least is a lot, if public money is involved. Over-all student numbers, for example, and hence admissions policy; special courses, including the provision of professional training; non-duplication of specialized topics; library resources; salaries; the provision of adequate scholarships and bursaries; research and its findings. One could multiply this list many times. Many aspects of all these questions are capable of local handling, and should so be handled. But all of them are problems about which the public at large is entitled to have an opinion, and it is reasonable to expect the government to develop policy in several of them—i.e., to assess the public need, and to expect the university system to provide for that need.

Yet in only one of these questions is there any long history of public involvement, and that is in professional education, notably in medicine, law and teaching. In most others Canada and her provinces have been singularly slow to establish strong requirements. This, of course, reflects a formerly colonial position. Canada has always been able, at a pinch, to import skilled manpower, capital and technologies, primarily from Britain and the United States. She has never been driven for any length of time upon her own resources. The long history of active planning of higher education in Britain and France reflects the opposite assumption: that the system must provide all the skills needed on the domestic market, and still have a surplus available for export to the less sophisticated countries—the imperial conscience, if you will. But Canada is no longer colonial, nor France and Britain imperial. Hence these assumptions are anachronisms. There are still distinguished Canadians who do not recognize colonialism when they see it, nor do they realize that colonialism is nowadays not imposed by others, but by oneself. I hesitate to quarrel with Ted Sheffield, who knows much more about Canadian education than I shall ever do, nor would I dream of accusing him of colonialism. But I can't accept his view that Canada ought to go on depending on imported university teachers. He is reported to have said:

We are not depending on the production of our own graduate schools, much less on the production of doctorates in our own graduate schools, to staff the universities—not wholly. . . . We are depending, have depended, will depend and I think, can successfully depend, on sources outside the country, not just of immigrants, but of Canadians who go abroad and then come back to serve in their own institutions.[16]

The long neglect of Canada's universities by an indifferent society guarantees that this is a statement of fact. But I also feel that it is intolerable, especially now that society is at last blessing our efforts. Canada is a rich nation, with a per capita income about three-quarters of that of the United States, and much greater than those of Britain and France. It should be a national objective to be able to meet

---

16. E. F. SHEFFIELD, quoted by Hon. William Davis, see footnote 11. After my lecture was over Dr. Sheffield was good enough to telephone his congratulations. My thanks are due to him for not boxing my ears!

all reasonable national requirements internally, and to be in a position to export both graduates and technology. Canada exports them both now, on a small scale, but falls short of meeting her own requirements. Of course it is good that she should staff her universities with returning Canadians; of course it is good that many non-Canadians should come here, too, because the university world ought to be international, or even supranational. But to rely on imported staff is a defensible policy only if one strives towards greater self-sufficiency, as do the Americans and the British, so as to be able to go on sending Canadian scholars abroad, where they are badly needed. May I say parenthetically how welcome they are in Britain, and how well they do there. Every college and university has them, and could do without them only with a real loss of versatility.

Here, then, is what one needs to plan. One has to bring the university systems to the point where they can meet and exceed national requirements in skilled manpower, in technical skills, in ideas and humane scholarship, and in intellectual advance. Reaching this point means a host of things. It means, obviously, providing places for all qualified undergraduate applicants, and this the Canadian university systems are tackling, with the help of public investment. But it is not enough to think simply in numbers. The next stage in Canada's academic history must be one of sophistication. This implies the enriching of physical resources, above all libraries, and specialized laboratories. It calls for the proliferation of graduate schools, and for a great widening in perspectives in advanced study. It presupposes the creation of facilities for Canada's professional education, a spectrum that will broaden rapidly in all Western countries, but especially in rich Canada. I hope that the universities will accept this latter responsibility, because I dislike professional education divorced from universities.

Canada will not get what I have just spelled out without a formal organization to plan it. Her constitution requires that this planning be provincial. Hence there is a need, in every province, but especially in Québec and Ontario, for a body charged with the over-all responsibility of planning university development. And the main force of my remarks is that the body should be itself academic in character, though not exclusively so. It must enjoy the full support of both government and the academic community, and it has to be given the powers and the resources necessary for the job. The questions that remain are these. What sort of body will fill this rôle? And what will happen to university freedom in such a planned system?

No system, other than that of complete centralization, can survive if the state does not want it to. All I can urge at present is that the universities should combine, federate, put their houses in order: and face the state with a reasonably clear conscience. You will see in my next talk that I incline towards statutory or constitutional arrangements rather than those dependent on convention. If the

31

niceties of polite upbringing are gradually failing the British, what hope is there in red-blooded Canada for such a system?

And what, finally, is to happen to these splendid new campuses in Canada? What will happen to their freedom to arrange their affairs as they think best? My fear is that it will die ingloriously. Reluctance to plan, to combine, may force the provinces to take over. But the hour is still not too late in Ontario, though it seems to be too early in Québec. Those who do not hang together hang separately. And whatever fate the Canadian university community may deserve, it doesn't deserve to be hanged.

2

REMEDIES

In my first talk I tried to make four points: that most universities now depend overwhelmingly on the state for funds; that this dependence means that the state-supported universities in any one jurisdiction have to be treated as a system; that someone has to run this system; and that the academic community, and not the state, should run it. I also said that I hoped that we could find a formula that would allow a measure of real freedom to the individual university. These were laboured and unoriginal thoughts. As David Munroe always says, the more important education becomes, the more boring it seems to get.

In my second talk I have to look at possible ways of running a university system. We have many good examples. The universities of Britain are a homogeneous system, and their development and operation are centrally financed and co-ordinated. Yet they possess individually a measure of real freedom, which they exercise vigorously. The nine large state universities of California form another centralized system. They, too, possess far more local autonomy than is usually believed. And both systems—British and Californian—obviously achieve high standards, meet public demands, and are good places to work and study in. I say this in spite of the current unrest at Berkeley and the London School of Economics. Before we speculate on proper Canadian remedies, then, I propose to look at some contrasted systems, in the hope of getting useful ideas. My experience of American systems is much thinner than of the British. This will become obvious as I speak.

What I did *not* say, but which I say now, is that the external threat to university freedom does not come from the state alone, even in its guise as financier. Society as a whole may threaten us, by putting demands on us that we cannot legitimately meet. I propose to dispose of the state first—I wish it was as easy as that—and keep the broader social influences for a depressing end to my depressing talks.

In my first talk I said that the device of the buffer committee—a body between government and university to whom the problem of finance is remitted—had two poles: the British soft-shoe concept of a self-effacing committee, and the American drum-roll concept of a Board of Regents. I may be wrong in suggesting that these are really opposite poles of a single planetary device; but at least they lie in the same domain: the no-man's-land between state and university.

The British University Grants Committee has achieved real fame and honour. I work under its wing, but I see it through Canadian eyes, since almost my whole previous career has been in Canada. I see much to admire: sophistication, modesty, common sense; and also some things to criticize, such as a very elaborate procedure for control of building projects. But most of all I see an idea characteristically British, attuned to the power structure of British public affairs, and assuming to the full the unwritten conventions on which British public life depends. Frankly, I doubt the exportability of this sort of thing—but the Committee has done so well that we must look at it attentively.

In its present form it dates back to 1919. It was the creation of a Canadian, Mr. Bonar Law, then Chancellor of the Exchequer, though similar committees had functioned back to 1889. The actual process involved was the circulation of a Treasury minute proposing the creation of a standing University Grants Committee "to enquire into the financial needs of university education in the United Kingdom [now Great Britain] and to advise the Government as to the application of any grants that may be made by Parliament towards meeting them." The Chancellor appointed a committee of nine academics, who reported not to the Board of Education, but to the Treasury. Thus began a long alliance between Committee and Treasury that lasted until 1964.[1]

---

1. University Grants Committee, *University Development 1957–1962* (London: H.M.S.O., Cmnd. 2267, 1964), 230 pp. Paragraphs 517–628, pp. 170–99, give a succinct summary of the Committee's history and working methods. For more recent developments see House of Commons, *Fifth Report from the Estimates Committee, Session 1964–65* (London: H.M.S.O., 1965), 288 pp. This rather critical assessment of the Committee's work was based on prolonged public hearings. Pp. v–xli contain the report proper. Pp. 1–280 contain the expert evidence *verbatim*, including memoranda from the Department of Education and Science and the U.G.C. itself. The Estimates Committee recommendations, pp. xlii-xliii, were referred to the Department of

On April 1st of that year—April Fools' Day—the Committee passed to the Department of Education and Science, whose Secretary of State today appoints the U.G.C., receives its reports, and speaks for it in the Commons.

The U.G.C. is thus not statutory, and the Minister can vary its membership and terms of reference. The latter now have added to them the responsibility "to collect, examine and make available information relating to university education throughout the United Kingdom; and to assist, in consultation with the universities and other bodies concerned, the preparation and execution of such plans for the development of the universities as may from time to time be required in order to ensure that they are fully adequate to national needs." The Chairman and the two Deputy Chairmen are salaried officials, the former full-time, the two deputies part-time, and carry an enormous responsibility. Of the remaining eighteen members, at a recent count, eleven are academics, two are persons connected with other forms of education, four are from industry, and one is from a research establishment. Each serves for a five-year term, renewable for a second five years.

Education and Science for comment and these comments (providing a useful footnote) are in House of Commons, *Third Special Report from the Estimates Committee Session 1965–66* (London: H.M.S.O., 1965), 8 pp. The tide flows quickly, as one learns in reading *Parliament and Control of University Expenditure: Special Report from the Committee of Public Accounts, Session 1966–67*, House of Commons Paper 290 (London: H.M.S.O., 1967).

There are numerous standing sub-committees and advisory panels, as well as *ad hoc* independent committees made up of non-members of the U.G.C. A secretariat (including architects) of over one hundred civil servants functions in support in Park Crescent (an elegant Regency terrace) far from the Secretary of State's offices in Mayfair.

Upon this deliberately self-effacing group of citizens the Government leans for advice about all university requirements, capital and operating (nonrecurrent and recurrent in U.G.C. language). Having decided on the amount of the grant to be made, the Government thereafter by firm convention allows the U.G.C. to distribute it in block grant form to the universities on its list. The process is described by Sir John Wolfenden (personal communication) as a "series of recommendations (by the U.G.C.) which in relation to recurrent grant are always accepted, never questioned and recognized . . . as wholly within our unquestioned discretion." The U.G.C. attempts to see that the universities spend the money wisely, but no further public audit is attempted. Operating grants are made quinquennially, with built-in adjustment factors, and with occasional supplementary grants to cover changes in salary scales, the setting up of new programmes and other unforeseen changes. Capital grants are dealt with continuously, and are made after scrutiny by the Committee's own architects and quantity surveyors. Neither the Comptroller and Auditor-General nor the Parliamentary Committee of Public Accounts has in the past had access to the Committee's books, nor to those of the universities. The Committee of Public Accounts has repeatedly attempted to set aside this provision, but the Treasury has supported the right of the universities to keep their books closed. To realize the force of the provision, try to visualize Mr. Watson Sellars, at the height of his career, or Mr. Maxwell Henderson today, being denied access to the books of one of the largest spenders of public funds, finding their way barred not only by the spender but by the officials of the Treasury Board. The Public Accounts Committee has finally thrust down this barrier, the Commons having voted to accept from January 1, 1968, their recommendation that both U.G.C. and university books be audited by the Auditor-General. So ends a long fight between the academic David and the Goliath of the state—with this Goliath invincible.[2]

The system has shown increasing signs of strain as the scale of public expenditure has risen. The process whereby new buildings are designed, authorized, built, and equipped strikes my Canada-conditioned eyes as slow and excessively elaborate. The public purse is protected, but it takes a year or two to complete what in Québec we should have finished in a few months. In its anxiety to justify the trust

---

2. For a review of the earlier history of this conflict, see ROBERT O. BERDAHL, *British Universities and the State* (Berkeley and Los Angeles: University of California Press, 1959), pp. 117–34. For the last act, see *Parliament and Control of University Expenditure: Special Report from the Committee of Public Accounts, Session 1966–67*, House of Commons Paper 290 (London: H.M.S.O., 1967).

put in it the Committee has felt it had no choice, on the capital side, but to put protection of the public purse high on its list of obligations. The London colleges (for example) cannot hope to do what government departments do with impunity as regards site and building acquisition in that most expensive city. It is only fair to say that the delays reside at least as much in the offices of the architects, surveyors, and lawyers employed by the universities, and on the building sites themselves, as in the overloaded offices of the U.G.C. It is the elaborateness of the system, with its laborious protection of one aspect of the public interest, that slows matters down, not any lack of competence or goodwill.

The Committee is expected to plan academic development in the national interest. This planning they have done by methods that again presuppose the British atmosphere in public affairs. They unobtrusively saw to it, for example, that proposals for new universities in post-war Britain were handled with proper regard for site, public needs, finances, and academic structure. The eight new institutions, though most of them were conceived and sponsored locally, all bear the mark of this forethought. Academic planning boards were set up in each case to ensure that the new universities were from the outset national institutions comparable with the older universities in standards. These planning boards were made up of a chairman and five or six members, all but one nationally respected academics. They were charged with making sure that the new university would be capable of awarding respectable degrees, and with determining the range of subjects that were to be taught at undergraduate level in the early years. They drafted the charters, and in consultation with the local sponsors selected the first governing bodies. They also helped find the first vice-chancellors. Thus the new universities, though refreshingly unlike one another, enjoy the respect of their academic colleagues. The success of places like Sussex speaks well for the effect of the background presence of the U.G.C.

I have stressed several times the unobtrusiveness of this background presence. There is much argument about the merits of *dirigisme*, or, as Ashby calls it, crypto-dirigisme,[3] by the U.G.C. In fact academic evolution in Britain is a most complex process. The U.G.C., by appointing *ad hoc* independent committees, can assess the public need, can advertise the results, and then (in principle) await proposals from the universities. In practice initiatives may flow from government, from the Committee of Vice-Chancellors and Principals, from individual universities, from non-academic bodies, or from the U.G.C. itself. The point is, however, that with minor exceptions financial provision will depend on U.G.C. approval. Thus academic development stands or falls by their decision, in practice if not in principle. Universities file their development proposals with the U.G.C. quinquennially. If the opinion of the Committee is negative, then the proposals will probably not go forward, because the

---

3. See TUDOR DAVID's account of an informal discussion held at Cambridge July 16–18, 1965, on "Government and University," *Minerva*, IV, (1) 1965–66, pp. 111–21.

universities, though protected from budgetary line-item control by the block grant principle, cannot afford to resist U.G.C. opinion, and may not even want to. Hence Ashby's term "crypto-dirigisme."

Is this Committee the voice of the academic community of Britain? The answer must clearly be no. It is in the main an agent of the state, fulfilling a public duty. The duty requires it, *inter alia*, to act as the agent of the corporate universities in dealing with the state. As Ashby and Anderson put it, "The *de facto* situation in Britain is that there is, of course, an unwritten concordat between university and state, through the medium of the University Grants Committee: one side acknowledges and accepts some measure of state influence and control; the other side agrees to a rigorous code of non-intervention in the university's academic affairs."[4] Bagehot would have comprehended this arrangement, though he would have been surprised that the "medium" should be dominated by academics.

The British universities have long felt the need for some form of mutual consultation, for some kind of collective voice. No formal organization has been set up for this purpose, and few have been bold enough to suggest that one with teeth is needed. The Committee of Vice-Chancellors and Principals, referred to a moment ago, dates from 1913, and is an active if rather mysterious body meeting monthly.

---

4. ERIC ASHBY and MARY ANDERSON, "Autonomy and Academic Freedom in Britain and in English-speaking Countries of Tropical Africa," *Minerva*, IV (3), Spring 1966, pp. 317–64.

It neither claims nor in fact possesses any authority. In practice it is becoming rapidly more influential, and steps are being taken to strengthen its hand. It now possesses a secretariat, and puts out occasional publications and sponsors studies of the university scene. Its chairman is in close touch with the chairman of the U.G.C. Sir John Wolfenden has gone on record that he dines with the chairman of the Vice-Chancellors' Committee the night before their monthly meeting, so that they may talk about the Vice-Chancellors' agenda items, "and," he adds, "this is understood among the Vice-Chancellors as a sensible way of exchanging views."[5] In a mad world, it seems a refreshingly sane procedure.

There will, I am sure, be a great expansion of this form of co-ordination in Britain in the coming years of dependence on government. Inevitably the University Grants Committee comes to be seen more and more as the voice of the state; equally inevitably, as their dependence on the state increases, the universities will have to learn to speak with a common voice, and to keep their common house in order. In my view the present Committee of Vice-Chancellors and Principals can well be the nucleus of such a co-ordinating body, though consultation at other levels will be necessary. In some few universities the vice-chancellor may not be accepted as a suitable voice for the academic body, and it may be that a more democratically conceived

---

5. Testimony cited in House of Commons, *Fifth Report from the Estimates Committee, Session 1964–65* (see note 1, chapter II), p. 261.

committee will be needed.[6] What I am sure of is that some such body will have to take hold of the university community in Britain and make sure that as a system it can speak clearly in its own collective interest.

I am not competent to speak with equal knowledge of American methods in these questions. Here, in any case, genuinely autonomous private universities persist, and are likely to persist for many years. This we all should welcome. But even in the United States many students must seek their education in publicly financed universities. State university systems are as characteristic of American culture as are the Ivy League and Rice University. Private and public can even co-exist, as do Stanford, the California Institute of Technology, and the University of California. The British and Ontario pattern of heavily state-subsidized yet private, autonomous universities is not so familiar to Americans, who have tended to keep institutions for the privileged separate in their minds from institutions for the multitude. Yet Cornell began as a land-grant college under the Morrill act, and there are many cases where the complex reality of American education differs from the stereotypes: not least at the University of Pennsylvania, private and proud of it, yet deriving two-fifths of its annual revenues from the Commonwealth legislature.

Most public university systems of the sort we

---

6. Committee on Higher Education (LORD ROBBINS, chairman), *Higher Education* (London: H.M.S.O., Cmnd. 2154, 1963), paras. 695–700.

have been discussing lack the appearance of autonomy retained by the British universities. A state university sees autonomy, or in more general terms freedom, as something to be wrung from a powerful parent, the state: it is not something it is in danger of losing, but something it has to gain. Annual line budgets that have to be accepted by the state legislature are still required in some states. Yet both the personal freedom of the teacher and the freedom of action of his university have in practice been growing. Chancellor Herman B. Wells of Indiana University, for example, points out that "the late Professor Kinsey served for many years on our faculty vigorously expounding ideas on sexual behaviour in conflict with the generally accepted mores of our society." And Chancellor Wells enjoys annual block grants.[7]

In fact, of course, as Wells points out, the current trend of university financing in the United States is in the opposite direction to that in Canada and Britain; dependence on a single public source is lessening in the United States. Massive federal subsidies to research have transformed the budgets of many of the state universities, as well as enriching the private. This federal support in the case of Indiana now amounts to a third of the total annual income of the University. Most of this support has been one-sidedly scientific, coming from the Na-

7. HERMAN B. WELLS, "United States of America," in *University Autonomy, Its Meaning Today* (Paper 7; Paris: International Association of Universities, 1965), pp. 125–28.

tional Science Foundation and the military services. Recently, however, the Congress authorized the establishment of a Council and Endowment for the Humanities, to be directed by Barnaby C. Keeney (who chaired the Commission on the Humanities that pulled off this *coup*). If I know Keeney and his associates the flow of money into humane studies will increase far beyond its present proportions.[8] Thanks partly to these large federal subventions the state universities have become rapidly more sophisticated and more versatile, especially in the past decade. Indeed it has become progressively more difficult to maintain their traditional rôle as teachers of the undergraduate hordes.[9] Getting money from more than one source of funds is a key to independence, and in the progressive states this diversification has been marked by increasingly wise action by state governments as regards the public universities. The latter have thus extended their freedom to plan without arbitrary interference.

In several of the richest states, real sovereignty rests with the Board of Regents of the state university system, who have jurisdiction in the name of the people over all the campuses of the system, though these may enjoy in practice a degree of autonomy almost as effective as that of the British

8. Commission on the Humanities (BARNABY C. KEENEY, chairman), *Report* (New York, 1964), 222 pp.

9. MARTIN TROW, "The Undergraduate Dilemma in Large State Universities," *Universities Quarterly*, 21 (1), December, 1966, pp. 17–43.

universities. Patterns vary greatly. In some states the Regents are elected by general suffrage; in others they may be appointed by the Governor. Americans put much less faith than do the British in unwritten conventions. The "unwritten concordat between university and state" I spoke of a little while ago does not appeal to a nation used to legal process and the separation of powers between judiciary, executive, and legislature. The strongest systems are built right into the state constitution. Thus in California, which has a state system with fully evolved campus autonomy, the Board of Regents own and operate the system under the 1879 Constitution of the state and are free of political control.[10] The state university contains nine individual universities and three colleges, as well as research institutions. The Regents command great respect; they include eight *ex-officio* members and sixteen distinguished laymen appointed by the Governor for sixteen-year terms. These western aristocrats present a unified budget to the legislature, which can reduce the total request (not below the previous year's appropriation) but cannot challenge any line items.[11]

Clearly these Regents exercise most of the functions which in Britain fall to the U.G.C., yet they are laymen, except for the President of the system,

10. Recent events suggest that they are not free from politics! What is wrong in California is not the structure, but the policies followed.

11. I am quoting here from Appendix H of the *Spinks Report* (see footnote 2, chapter I). Governor Reagan's recent irruption seems to have ignored this provision.

who is a voting member. The provision that the Regents should be a lay body reflects the deep-seated differences between assumptions in the United States and in the United Kingdom as to proper government. At times it has led to tension between the academic staff and the Regents—and their recent difficulties with the Berkeley students are in all of our minds. Similarly the Regents' constitutional status and guarantees are quite alien to British politics. Functionally similar, the two kinds of body are thus constitutionally very different.

State Boards of Regents exercise, by means of committees, full control of academic policies, but these committees, of which the senior is often called a Senate, are academic bodies, and by convention— here the practice is more familiar to British eyes— the academic policy of the system is determined here. The heterogeneity of the American university community, where lame ducks waddle alongside racing thoroughbreds, makes academic opinion acutely conscious of varying standards, and of the need for accreditation, especially of professional and graduate programmes. Hence the Regents of a state university system habitually exercise through their academic committees much wider power than the British would stomach. The right of authorization for expensive Ph.D. programmes, or for new professional schools, typically lies with the Regents themselves, as in California. In Britain this right lies with the individual university, although that right will be subject to U.G.C. consent if increased costs are involved.

What, then, should Canadians do? Ought they to

borrow ideas from the British or from the Americans, and try to adapt them? Ought they conceivably to borrow from France? Or should they borrow what is good and then work out their own solution?

Before I give you an answer, let me speculate a bit about Canada's special problems. These are very numerous, and some of them look almost insoluble, such as staffing her universities with native sons. All have a bearing on cost, and hence raise the question of state support, federal or provincial.

The first problem is the question of scale, and its consequences. The decision has been taken in nearly all provinces to provide university places for all who can profit. And the latter term has been interpreted generously. The lower third of all students entering the Canadian universities are marginal for such education. I don't wish to be too precise about this, but we all know that a high proportion—in some places a half—of those who enter do not graduate. In Britain, by contrast, all but 10 to 20 per cent will get a first degree. This difference reflects the greater ease with which the young Canadian gets to college: he lives in a country with an open-door policy, whereas the British characteristically filter more drastically. They set higher minimum requirements, and then reject half the qualified applicants. In the result, a disturbingly high fraction of Canadian university expenditure—and of the energy and patience of teachers—is partially wasted by being spent on those unable to profit from this level of education. Of course something rubs off, but not, I suspect, much. The British get round this waste by setting up a second tier of colleges—technical and teacher-training—administered by local authorities. The less well qualified in general find their way into this lower tier of what is usually called the binary system. The U.G.C. and universities have nothing to do with these colleges. The latter offer some degree courses (the degrees are granted externally by the University of London, or else supervised by the new National Council for Academic Awards), but devote themselves primarily to less demanding work. Canadian university systems try to cover both functions, as do the state universities in the United States. The two-tier structure of the binary system offends my own prejudices, and I accept that the North American formula is ultimately the sounder. Nevertheless gathering so wide a spectrum of intelligence inside a single system creates major problems for Canada. It commits the provinces to costly provision for very large numbers, in a country that until recently starved its universities, and hence allowed them to reach our own day desperately short of buildings, staff, and facilities. I would not wish to change the national open door policy: but it does pose problems.

High among these is the obsession with numbers, staff–student ratios, wastage, student aid, and all the paraphernalia of a mass-education approach. Discussions of academic policy are mainly about these things.[12] How, that is, to cope with the

12. Advisory Committee on University Affairs of Ontario, *Report* (Toronto, Feb. 1, 1964).

oncoming mass of school-leavers within a single equalitarian framework. Hence one argues about, for example, junior colleges, or institutes (as the Parent Commission preferred) as a means of taking the pressure off the huge classes of early university years.[13] And one hears, in Québec and Ontario at least, and in some quarters in British Columbia, of another two-tier idea: that of advanced universities dealing primarily with honours and graduate work, and of work-a-day liberal arts colleges for the run-of-the-mill entrant who only seeks a meek-and-mild general degree. This idea also offends me, and I think it incapable of being carried out. My own conviction is that all "two-tier" arrangements are unsound. If you set up a university system, it must be made up of self-respecting universities. The liberal arts college was a creation of an earlier phase of American education; and locally (though in my view rarely) it achieved distinction (for example at Dartmouth or at Antioch).[14] But now-a-days teaching has to be done alongside research, if it is to carry conviction. And research means university status, as that term is now commonly used. It is not enough, in thinking about the expansion of

13. Royal Commission of Inquiry on Education in the Province of Québec, *Report* (Québec, 1964), II, 176–90, paras. 283–301.

14. I should record the strong dissent of the Hon. G. O. Arlt from this opinion! He reminds me that there were many such centres of distinction, but agrees that many of them have now moved on to graduate programmes.

universities, simply to calculate in terms of numerical formulae, of bodies and of floor-space: you have to think about how to keep your standards abreast of the next fellow's—and in Canada's case he is painfully close!

Hence I would put second among the special problems that of sophistication. The Canadian universities exist side by side on this continent with the American universities. It has been possible in the past for Canadians to feel smug about their academic standards. Honours graduates have found a ready welcome across the border in the American graduate schools, and have been able to compete on equal or even advantageous terms. Even the general graduate has often found his feet. It has therefore been easy for Canadians to ignore the great changes that are being carried through on the American campus, and to assume that Canada had some innate quality that kept her ahead of her neighbours in the undergraduate school.

This comfortable feeling has nothing to justify it. The American willingness to condemn American institutions—loud self-denunciation is part of their way of life—obscures the facts. I have no objective way of proving my conviction, held against highly vocal American opinion to the contrary, that the high school leaver in the United States is far better equipped for university life than he was ten years ago, and that the undergraduate schools now reflect that better equipment; but I am sure of this. We should add the great capital investment that has been going on everywhere. Altogether the American university now seems to me in my frequent visits a much more exciting place than it used to be. I am not just talking about Harvard, M.I.T., Chicago, and Stanford, but about the state university systems. Where in Canada is there a phenomenon like Michigan State at East Lansing? Or like much-maligned Berkeley? The fact is that Canadian universities are competing against the most vigorous and exciting universities in existence: and they *must* compete on adequate terms.

By sophistication I mean simply creating the graduate schools, the libraries, the research laboratories, the specialized institutes that are now standard parts of the great university, and increasingly even of the hitherto humdrum state university in the United States. In Canada we have Toronto, we have McGill, we have exciting beginnings elsewhere: we have small pools of real excellence. But only Toronto is yet within striking distance of world stature—because of imaginative leadership, large public financial support, and a very early start (by Canadian standards). McGill has great potential, too, but has sometimes been hamstrung by the short-sightedness of the provincial government. I mean no idle courtesy when I say that your beginnings here at Carleton are impressive and exciting. But you need vastly more resources and time.

You will not expect me to repeat the findings of the Spinks Commission. I will only say that we believed that every university in the province of Ontario must move rapidly towards advanced work: the master's degree everywhere, the doctorate where resources justify it. We rejected the view that some of these universities could be kept out of the advanced field; we believed that there is no way of putting a lid on scholarship, and that a university is either free to go as far as the intellect can, or it is not a university at all. And I believe this to be true also of the rest of Canada's universities. Notably it is true of Québec, and the Parent Commission's view that only the big three—McGill, Laval, Montréal—should currently do graduate work is questionable.[15]

But having said all this, I must re-emphasize the grimness of the job of getting the Canadian universities into better shape for advanced work. Let me isolate one problem from among the crowd: library resources. The Spinks Commission estimated (on the basis of recognized standards) that the libraries of the Ontario universities were about 600,000 volumes below standard for their undergraduate programmes, and nearly 5,000,000 volumes below the standard required for graduate work in those universities *that had already begun such work.* Turned crudely into dollars, these figures imply a capital grant requirement of about $85,000,000 to bring the libraries up to standards similar to those already aimed at in the better American systems. Such calculations should not be taken too seriously.

---

15. Royal Commission of Inquiry on Education in the Province of Québec, *Report* II, 232, para. 349. What the Commissioners recommended was that the other universities should refrain from exercising their charter powers to do graduate work for a few years.

The real cost might be half, or it might be double. But, half or double, it remains a shocking figure.

Here, to me, is the real rub. We have not only to meet social demand for university places. We have also to diversify, enrich, and ennoble the universities so that they are not inferior to their neighbours. This is another reason why it is crucially necessary for the government of every province to take good advice about its university system—and to find resources to accept it. That advice must come from the academic community itself, not exclusively, but in the main. Which brings us back again to the theme of university and government in Canada.

First of all we might agree that solutions have got to be found quickly. Fully satisfactory arrangements do not yet seem to exist anywhere. I make these remarks tentatively, because I have not followed Duff and Berdahl across the country, and must rely on more casual contacts. In Québec the situation is, and has been, disquieting: prolonged indecision as to mechanics has led to deep frustration and unease throughout the university community, in both cultural groups; the 1967 provincial budget is financially more generous, but leaves the mechanics still up in the air. Here in Ontario respectable and obviously well-intentioned initiatives by the provincial government have still not created a fully satisfactory scheme. Nowhere in Canada, least of all in Québec and Ontario, should this situation be tolerated much longer. Since I am partially an outsider I apologize for thus seeming to poke my nose in. But the whole academic world, inside and outside Canada, has a stake in your success: so I hope you will forgive me for beating the drum.

The answer preferred by most Canadian academics, and seemingly acceptable to most politicians, is the provincial advisory committee, often modelled to a great extent on what is thought to be British practice. Such committees already exist in most provinces. But the British U.G.C., as we have seen, is non-statutory, and depends for its success on the conventions of British public life. These have no force in Canada, whose own ideas on proper government are very different. The common convention of Canadian provincial politics is that office means power, subject only to the constraints of the law, and to the vote of the legislature. It is asking a lot to have politicians delegate this huge and vital job of planning a university system to others, and refrain, in the face of ever-increasing cost, from using that power to interfere. Frankly I don't think their restraint will last without guarantees. But since these committees already exist in many provinces, let me suggest a few things about their functioning.

First, the committees must be respected by both legislature and academic community. This means careful thought as to membership. I don't believe that high permanent officials should serve, nor should active politicians. Ideally, I would put my faith in a combination of three elements, with provision for rotation in all cases: prominent lay members, with sympathy for university objectives; heads of universities (presidents make more trouble off

57

than on such committees); and senior professors. I prefer an academic majority, but do not feel that this matters if you pick a good team. There should certainly be, among the laymen, representatives of the school system, including at least one high school principal or senior teacher. In all this I find I am agreeing with Duff and Berdahl.[16]

Secondly, in the absence of comfortable conventions, I advocate a statutory rôle for such committees, with well-articulated terms of reference built into the legislation. These should include the right, *the exclusive right*, to present annual operating budgets for the system to the appropriate Ministers; the right, again exclusive, to co-ordinate plans for new developments (including new professional schools), and hence to present annual capital budgets to the Ministers; the right to distribute these monies to the universities as they think just, and to arrange suitable systems of audit.

Thirdly the committees must have a secretariat, complete with technical staff sufficient to do the assessment, scrutiny, control, and audit required by the job. The substantial bureaucracies now existing in departments of higher education should more properly work for the committee than for the Minister. One bureaucracy or two is a question that still divides Britain. Since major commitments of capital are always fought out at ministerial level it is natural that the Minister responsible for university finance should want his team of advisers: but if the

---

16. *Duff-Berdahl Report* (see footnote 7, chapter I), pp. 76–82.

committee is to do its job and preserve the freedom of the universities, much of the work now done in Canada by departmental bureaucracies will have to be done by the staffs of the committees. One bureaucracy or two, however, let me plead for the minimum of niggling control. Universities are highly responsible bodies, governed by people with strong social consciences, staffed by the intelligent and the dedicated. It is patent nonsense to insist on pettifogging detail of financial control over such bodies. My experience is that such control is more likely to strangle us than any conscious attack on our freedom. So, in heaven's name, let us keep one publicly financed domain out of the reach of red tape.[17]

Fourthly, the operating budgets of the universities simply must be guaranteed several years ahead. The present process of annual budgeting is inefficient, frustrating, and costly. It commits the senior staff of all universities, and of the committees, to a futile annual rat-race. As dean of a faculty of thirty-odd departments I spent much of the year telling my senior colleagues that I could give them no commitments on anything—until, in fact, it was too late. The British use a quinquennial system, which I think too long. Personally I favour a revisable three-year system for Canadian jurisdictions, and am not impressed by arguments that it is politically unfeasible. Since it is a necessity for good university governance it has got to be made feasible.[18]

---

17. See TUDOR DAVID (footnote 3, chapter II).

18. I part company from the *Duff-Berdahl Report* at this point (their p. 81).

Now, if this is what you want in Canada, and you can get these conditions met, there is an important corollary. Such committees must function as agents of the provinces. However academic they may be in composition they represent the public interest, not the special interest of the university community. The latter also needs a voice. Hence I repeat what I have said twice before: the universities must learn to speak with a common voice, and must keep their own houses in order. They need an inter-university organization with teeth. Committees of Presidents are not nearly enough. I have already spoken of how angular individualism and intense local academic nationalisms make academics fight shy of combination. But British experience shows that such combination is inevitable when one is faced with the state. Personally I am an out-and-out federalist. Birkbeck College is a member of a federal university, and gains immensely from this sharing of interest with others. Of course we have lost some of our autonomy: we no longer have exclusive control over curricula, and if we want to start something expensive we have to convince the other members of the university, and that university's expert governing body, before our bill is sent to the U.G.C. But in fact we are very fairly treated, and the College's Board of Governors and Academic Board would certainly resist any attempt to dismember the federal structure. What is the use of autonomy if one starves for money and for students?

You all know that the Spinks Commission advocated for Ontario a stronger, more formal American pattern: a federated provincial university, with an academic senate and a board of regents, the first dealing with academic co-ordination and planning, the latter with finance.[19] The Commission thought that, armed with strong enabling legislation, such a body could reserve to the academic community the primary rôle in planning for the future. It did not advocate any amalgamation or dismantling of the existing universities, nor did it envisage any more loss of sovereignty than is, in fact, already almost lost. Imperial College and University College, the London School of Economics and Kings College have not suffered from membership in a federal university—in fact, the reverse. I am sure that the London colleges would be in a very much weaker position if they had individually, as fully autonomous institutions, to face the state through the University Grants Committee, though it is fair to add that some of the members, chiefly the large colleges, would like to have a go: there are rogue elephants in every herd. The Commissioners knew, of course, that they would tread on corns in recommending for Ontario as they did: and, frankly, they were more concerned that *something* should be done by their brother academics than that their own solutions should be chosen. There are other possible solutions, as I have tried to suggest tonight. But whichever pattern is adopted, my strictures about the necessary powers of the chosen instrument will stand.

In fact, however, the efficacy of these solutions—those discussed above, and others that may be

---

19. *Spinks Report*, pp. 77–82.

imagined—always depend on the answer to these simple questions: Is the state willing to accept the advice of the intermediary, whether advisory committee, Board of Regents, or U.G.C.? Is it willing to forgo the right of listening to other persuasive and influential voices? Will it give the bureaucratic job, which all admit is necessary, to the intermediary rather than to its own civil service? And will it appoint to the intermediary persons of such reputation that they cannot be ignored, by itself, by the universities, or by the public at large? If it will do these things, the exact mechanism probably doesn't matter, though I will not retreat from my preference for statutory instruments. As Kipling said of the Neolithic Age, "there are nine and sixty ways of constructing tribal lays, and every single one of them is right." But if the state does not wish to delegate the job, or if it does so half-heartedly, then university financing will remain a matter for heartburnings and recriminations; and the freedom of universities —even limited freedom—becomes a myth.

May I come now to another aspect of freedom? I see yet another threat in the financing of research. Research is not a pleasant frill to be added to the real business of a university, nor is it just an adjunct to undergraduate teaching. It is in fact the core of a university's work, and university financing that does not recognize this falsifies the facts. About half the operating costs of the British universities arise from the advancement of knowledge—research—and half from dissemination of that knowledge—teaching. These two functions are thus equally supported by the Exchequer Grant handled by the U.G.C., and they have never been separated, though costing exercises now in progress by the U.G.C. and the Committee of Vice-Chancellors and Principals involve such analysis.[20] Few Canadian jurisdictions yet admit this principle, which is fundamental to the freedom of the scholar, and to communities of scholars. Most Canadian justifications of budgets are in terms of the undergraduate teaching "load," and the universities are forced to lean on the National Research Council, the Canada Council, or other external bodies for the overt financing of research.

The idea that university financing should pay only for teaching is quite wrong. The general operating budget of all universities must allow for research costs, and general provincial support for academic research from the universities must therefore be to the institution, not the individual. The crucial rôle of the research councils, federal and provincial, should be to support the work of *individual* scholars or teams of scholars who wish to conduct research and to support students who wish to work for higher degrees. This duality contains a most important principle: that the individual member of the university needs to be able to finance his creative ideas independently of his institution's existing programmes. This essential freedom is the key to initiative and intellectual innovation. In my opinion all provinces, as well as the federal government, should

---

20. University Grants Committee, *University Development 1957–1962* (see footnote 1, chapter II), paras. 159–63, pp. 55–57.

have such research councils, with terms of reference covering all aspects of research. Without such separate right of access to sources of funds, the creative scholar may fall victim to the natural inertia of big organizations: and universities these days are very big indeed.

I wish I felt that I had by now spelt out the full list of threats to university freedom, and that I had been able to offer you safe remedies. But I see still other hazards. Universities belong in the wide-open world at large; they have to trade in ideas that possess no nationality, and they must hope to get their members, professor and student alike, from a world-wide constituency. Yet they must also serve their parent societies, on several scales. Carleton belongs to Ottawa, to Ontario, to Canada—but also (I'm embarrassed to say) to Western civilization. Carleton must often feel the conflict, and universities everywhere feel it. In the last analysis the real loyalties of universities are supra-national, yet they have to get their support from the individual state: and in Canada that mostly means in this context the provinces. Fortunately there are many signs that the legislators are coming to feel pride in the international rôle of Canada's universities: in the flood of students that come here from overseas, in the growing reputation of Canadian scientists, in the cosmopolitan atmosphere of the faculty clubs. Let's hope that this pride grows, and that no parochialism emerges.

And I mean, of course, parochialism inside as

well as outside the universities. There is no room for nationalism on the campus. It is right that a country should expect its universities to enrich the national store of knowledge, and to cultivate the things the nation does best. It is wrong to expect a university to take a paltry nationalistic view of the world. This has happened all too often in Europe, in Africa, in South America. It is right for a university to have its doors open to every shade of political, religious, intellectual, and artistic opinion, regardless of origin; wrong to espouse one view *institutionally*. It is right for a university in this country to lay emphasis on the two nearly identical cultures of the Western world, French and English, and to keep both doors open on every campus; wrong to voice vindictive criticism of one or the other on nationalist grounds. It is right to judge American culture on its merits, and to absorb those parts of it that are worthy of admiration; wrong to talk about "Americanization" as if that term had any consistent and prejudicial meaning. In other words Canadian universities must remember that their obligations, unlike their sources of funds, are anything but parochial.

3

WHOSE FREEDOM?

I have deliberately restricted my treatment to the second kind of academic freedom, to that enjoyed by the autonomous universities. This is a sort of collective freedom, a privilege granted to a large and complex community. Do we, in fact, think that this freedom extends to all members of the university? Or is it simply the privilege of the decision-makers? Or of the faculty?

These questions have got to be answered quickly if universities are to retain their autonomy. Internal bickering cannot be kept quiet. If faculty and governors disagree, or if there is an outcry among the students against the way things are run, the press will see to it that the external public knows. The universities have many critics, some of whom are delighted to use such disunity as a stick to beat academic heads with. In brief, if universities as corporate bodies are to be allowed to run their own affairs, they must run them well: and they must attempt, as did London's early underground railway steam locomotives, to consume their own smoke.

At present thick smoke is swirling up over one campus bush-fire. This is the question of staff–student relations, of Berkeleyism, of student activism. In many places, perhaps most, the English-speaking universities have apparently failed to convince their own students that their affairs are being run properly. Veritable sieges have been staged on both sides of the Atlantic, and the lives of senior campus administrators have become increasingly dominated by the demands of vocal, angry, and importunate student leaders. Historically there is nothing new about student unrest. What is new is that it is news, and that it shows signs of effective strategic planning. There are rumours of *agents-provocateurs* flitting from campus to campus, and there is a strong suspicion that the radical left is behind it all.

I confess that I am at a loss to account for the present pattern of unrest, and I have been too close to events to be able as yet to see them in perspective. Published comment so far is minimal, cautious, and often tendentious: there are few footnotes in this final section of my essay. I am suspicious of instant diagnoses of academic ailments. Yet I must comment, because I am certain that the autonomy of the universities will not survive an open conflict between students and "university authorities," however constituted. Already there are cries of outrage from politicians and other leaders of the community. At Berkeley, Clerk Kerr has been dismissed, following Governor Reagan's arrival among the trustees. In Britain the sit-in at the London School of Economics has brought acid comment about two things: first, the prominent rôle played by foreign students who are subsidized by the taxpayer, and second, the fact that most of the British students sitting in the entrance hall had local authority grants covering fees and maintenance. "Why," say the grumblers, "should the taxpayer subsidize these layabouts?"

The answer is, of course, that they are not just layabouts. I admit at once that among the student activists there are some very difficult people, young men and women to whom any sort of authority is anathema, any sort of compromise unwelcome; there are even some who have made a brief but hectic career out of a problem whose solution would send them back into obscurity. Equally there are, here and there, non-students who are seeking to manipulate the unrest for political advantage. But of the sincerity of the majority I have no doubt, nor do I question that we must answer their questioning.

I make a distinction here between the spill-over on to the campus of ban-the-bomb campaigns and political demonstrations of all sorts and discontent with the university system. The universities must steer clear of political partisanship, and leave such matters to the proper forums (in which, of course, their members may be as vocal as they wish). As long as the state concedes the ordinary liberties of democratic organization, the universities must refrain from corporate political action in non-educational matters. It is the objective of some of the student activists to overturn this principle, and to involve universities and academic organizations in direct political action. Thus the British National Union of Students faces within its own membership a new pressure group called the Radical Student Alliance that seeks to open up the Union's affairs to all classes of political activity. Such pressure must be opposed by those who want state-supported universities to retain their autonomy. Opposed, that is, in free, liberal societies. I might think otherwise in South Africa or Spain, because in neither country does the state concede the liberties within which such a policy is acceptable.

On the other hand, pressure from students for a greater say in university government, and their criticism of the way universities are run, must be listened to sympathetically and patiently. They are full members of most universities; the charters say that the members of the university shall include governors, faculty, graduates, and students. In justice we cannot deny that they, like other members, can have their opinions about both internal governance and external policy. If they believe, as many do, that they are excluded from both, and are subject to repressive regulations, to inefficient teaching, and to arbitrary discipline, they have got to be heard. It is an essential part of my thesis that the autonomy of universities shall be exercised by bodies whose whole membership feels itself adequately enfranchised.

How valid is the claim that there is widespread student discontent? At first sight there is no doubting it. The fires burn in many countries. But it only takes a few to make a lot of smoke. Student activists, like activists in any group, are a small minority. Ordinary union councils are elected by a small fraction of the electorate, and their greatest problem at general meetings is to raise and then retain a quorum. The mass of students remain obstinately inactive. If not contented, they succeed in containing their discontent. Hence student revolt has to be organized and led with great vigour. This is frustrating for its organizers, and no doubt accounts for the very bad manners shown by some.

But it would be quite wrong for university authorities to shield behind such a defence, because some of the charges laid against the universities by their students are at least arguable. The critics say that they are not properly taught and examined, especially if they are undergraduates; that the universities have become machines, lacking the warmth of personal contact; that the authorities do not allow the students to run their own unions and clubs autonomously; that the disciplinary codes are out of date, arbitrary, and paternalistic, and are not fairly applied; and that the students, though full members of the university, have no say in its government, which is remote from them. If justified, all of these criticisms are serious—though the last is highly controversial. Moreover they clearly bear on all students, and not just the torch-bearers.

The key charges are those concerning government and discipline, because these involve relations with the state and the legal obligations of the university. It can also be argued that the earlier charges—about poor teaching, unfair disciplinary procedures and others of the same cloth—arise because students are not involved in the internal governance of the universities: they have no constitutional route for protest. In practice this argument is a red herring. I am certain that most present-day students get what they want out of their universities, and are treated with every consideration by most of the staff, as was my generation. Nor do I believe that disciplinary injustice is common. Constitutional guarantees will in fact have only marginal influence on student life and prospects.

Nevertheless I take sides with those who call for reforms aimed at a greater degree of student involvement in university governance. I base my view on rather different grounds. Universities are highly conservative bodies. Left to themselves they tend to favour the *status quo ante*. Curricular change is a slow business, and the atmosphere of "hands off the departments" that dominates faculty and senate action works in practice towards conservatism. I am not saying that there are great weaknesses in the academic programmes of the Canadian universities, nor am I saying that they are more than usually conservative. They are more venturesome than their British cousins. It is, however, true that where change is needed, where the curriculum has got out of step with student needs, where the system has begun to creak and groan, then the internal governance of nearly all universities is ill equipped to put matters right quickly.

There are two devices for coping with such situations. One, sometimes used in Canada, is to commission external consultants, usually from other universities. These experts are invited to report on the situation, and to recommend change. Typically they take evidence on the campus, and they usually listen to student opinion. This method is of American origin, and some of the inter-university organizations, like the Council of Graduate Schools in the

74

United States, offer help in finding suitable consultants. Nevertheless this corrective device is hard for many to swallow: it looks like a confession of internal failure—which it often is—and it frequently involves only the substitution of one professorial opinion for another. On this view the solutions proposed are rarely radical enough, because the external consultants share the reticences, prejudices, and professional courtesies of the faculty.

The other device, more drastic and rarely attempted, is to give organized student opinion a voice, via the senate or governing body. I speak from experience: there are two students among the governors of Birkbeck College, where the tradition is more than a century old. Students also sit on several of the key committees, though not on the Academic Board (our Senate). The arrangement strikes me as splendid for Birkbeck, and it is fully accepted by all sections of the College. Experience predisposes me towards student involvement; I have seen it work in practice.

The great gain is that the students offer a corrective to the conservatism I have described. They are addicted to short-term solutions, to issues of principle. Compromise is apt to be a dirty word. One can rely on them to over-simplify issues, and not to be restrained, as the faculty is, by undue courtesy. And there is much to be said, in the complex world of the universities, for a little constructive over-simplification; in political affairs good policy depends on it. Much student comment, when given to reporters and other outsiders, is discourteous and aggrieved. Put the same spokesmen round a table and allow them to discuss the same grievances with the faculty or governors, and the sourness disappears. It is the sense that they will not be listened to that gives the tongues of the better students that rough, rasping sound.

There are many problems in bringing this participation off. Students sometimes elect representatives of extreme views, and there is no guarantee that the elected men will truly represent the general interest. Perhaps democracy is better served, in any case, if they follow the honourable practice of speaking their own minds, rather than the collective view of their own constituencies. And it is no joke to ask an active student to serve on academic committees. Why should we wish on to his shoulders time-wasting jobs we try to escape ourselves? In many universities there are now arrangements whereby union presidents get a paid sabbatical year, so heavy are their duties. To add membership of academic or governing bodies to the same men will really break their backs. The student doesn't really know his institution well enough, moreover, to serve sensibly until his senior or postgraduate years, and he can rarely serve for more than one or two years.

Precisely how and where you involve the students in governance will depend on your particular statutes and character. At places like Birkbeck College, where even the undergraduates are of average age 26 to 28, it makes good sense to put their representatives on the governing body. I doubt if this is sensible for ordinary undergraduate institutions. The

Duff-Berdahl report recommends that the students elect non-students to the Boards of Governors, thereby avoiding the presence of bewildered and overawed youngsters among the influential.[1] I don't see this as a solution, although graduate students or junior faculty who were undergraduates in the same university may possibly suffice.

It may be that the real place for the student representative is on the Senate, Academic Board or equivalent body, or on their committees. The proper business of a university is scholarship, and those aspects of policy that concern scholarship all come before the Senate. The anxieties of the student body about curriculum, examinations, and discipline are all debated there. Most students have very quaint ideas about what goes on at Governors' meetings (even the faculty has misconceptions). They are unaware that most if not all the decisions that directly concern them have long ago fallen to the Senate—and that Canadian Senates, by and large, have woken up with a vengeance and are now good bodies to attend. I don't, however, wish to dogmatize about these matters, because I feel uncertain myself, and sense uncertainty in other commentators, both staff and student.

I have recently attended a conference on staff–student relations organized by World University Service in London. It was an impressive occasion, on which representatives of the National Union of

---

1. *Duff-Berdahl Report* (see footnote 7, chapter I), pp. 65–67.

Students and various student unions sat down to argue with representatives of the universities and colleges of Britain (including the technical and teacher training colleges). To their surprise, I suspect—and certainly to mine—they found themselves applauding one another, not arguing. There was widespread agreement that the real crux is that the student body and the faculty should agree, and be in proper relation one to the other. Among those who spoke most eloquently was William Boyd, Vice-Chancellor for Student Affairs of the University of California at Berkeley. He pleaded that the universities of Britain should at all costs *listen* to student outcry. He told the conference that Berkeley activism had shifted its attack, first from central government to university administration, then from administration to academic policy. Student effort was now to shake loose, influence, even control the intellectual work of the university itself.

Few of us would want to go that far. Professors know much more about their fields than can their students, however gifted, and their relationship is not one of equality. The only equality is that of concern. This is enough to justify student membership of Senate or Senate committees. It is not enough to justify any abdication by the senior members of the university over intellectual standards.

It is much healthier that student activism should move in this direction than that it should try to make the university an instrument to remould society by political action. Of course the university remoulds society by its intellectual effort. The stream of graduates leaving its gates, the ideas it propagates, will ensure that end. And this is what the student can help to advance.

I have given my answer, right or wrong. It is to enfranchise the student in the right place and with the right objectives. The question "whose freedom" then loses its force, because the old paternalistic gap between teacher and taught is narrowed. I suggest this enfranchisement because I think it will be good for the universities. Turmoil, tension, and unease have always done us good. The present situation has its perils, but offers much greater opportunities. In Canada the tension comes at a time of extraordinary expansion. In Snow's words, it is a time of hope. To go with the new buildings, the new programmes, and the new race of students, Canada must move cautiously and pragmatically towards a more coherent academic community—whose collective freedom is what I seek.

Let me end by quoting that old and eloquent friend of university freedom, Monseigneur Lussier, former Recteur of the Université de Montréal. I heard him speak to a McGill Convocation, ten years ago. Our problem then was to persuade government to finance us. Ottawa had taken the plunge of federal aid, but we in Québec were not allowed to accept the grant; and provincial aid, in the dark ages of Duplessis, was exiguous and erratic. What we feared was starvation through public indifference. No one threatened our freedom, and no one seemed to work for our survival. Now the threat springs from the scale of public support. Can we stay free while we spend so much of the exchequer's money? It seems unlikely. But so, then, did the end of the Duplessis era: yet it was close at hand. So I close with Lussier's words, which he says he drew from William of Orange:

In the absence of hope
it is still necessary to strive.